A Twirly-Swirly Christmas
poems & prose

Shirley Richards

Copyright © 2021   Shirley Richards

All rights reserved.

Penney Publishing

penneywrites@gmail.com

ISBN:978-0-6450417-2-9 (paperback)
ISBN: 978-0-6450417-3-6 (eBook)

Dedicated to Jo
for her encouragement and fortitude
in this compilation of work

Tree of Hope

Surprisingly, or maybe as things stand of late with the delta scare, I may have inadvertently decided to leave the Christmas tree up as a token or symbol of hope.
Hope for a better year in 2021 or maybe it's a feeling that because Christmas 2020 was a bit of a fizzier I'm not taking it down as a type of protest, almost like I'm stretching Christmas over to make up for the non-Christmas of last year. It's the very first time in my 62 years as a home maker that the Christmas tree has been left up for a whole year.

I do have a large fibre-optic Christmas tree with lights and bling but I put up a small Christmas tree last year for the almost non-Christmas festivities. This year I'm bringing out the big guns with the flashing lights, then, I'll have one big Christmas tree and one small making it a real Christmas celebration with a winking, blinking, chameleon.

But I must add that life is so precious. It's well worth bearing up to a few snap lockdowns until Christmas if need be… so maybe that is why the tree of hope is still standing since 2020, as a sign of real healing-hope for me, my family, my friends and relations, and for everyone.

Hold onto hope, dear reader!

November 2021
Warrnambool, Vic
Australia

It's been there all year

No partridge
In a pear tree
No gold rings
No French hens
On the 2020th
Day of Christmas...
It's been there all year
It won't disappear
It looks a bit tired
There's no place
To hide
It's been there all year
There's no bling
There is no light
It's a miserable sight
It's been there all year
It won't disappear
No one looks twice
It's lost charm
It's not nice
It's been there all year
It won't disappear
You see it
Don't care
It's so old
Oh, not young.
New apparel
For some
Erases the glum
A wee bit of colour
Some highlights
And fake snow

Will brighten it up
Reinvent the old
Show
Overall white
Will bright and delight
Put last year's
To shame
Standing all year
The same
Like a dunce
In a corner
Facing blame
It's been there all year
It won't disappear
Unloved, unclaimed
The year was lost
Due to lockdowns
That cost
Covid unclear
Nothing to cheer
Some jobs done
Not so for some
Here's hoping
This Christmas
Will be open to fun
To outside with family
To mingle with some
So it's out with the old
In with the new
With hope...
For a very merry
Christmas
To everyone
From me

And the revamped
Christmas tree!

I Have The iPhone

(If) spending Christmas alone
Tho' I have the iPhone.
Got bbq chook- no need to cook
And an interesting new book.
My fur-baby's my guest
We'll be doing our best
To enjoy Christmas alone
And some ham off the bone
It's not the cat's whiskers
Being solo at Christmas
But, I have the iPhone
So, can FaceTime my own.
The family can't come
Got essentials hum-drum.
We're alone, but not out
To us there goes a shout out
I gulp down a champers
Then burp! The cat scampers
Then I'll watch Bad Santa
And enjoy his earthy banta
As I eat plum-duff and sauce
With brandy custard of course
Then take a nap in my chair
Feel contented not a care
Dreaming of family -
Wishing covid 2020 elsewhere!

A Christmas Picnic

Spraying begone to pesky insects
Bug-off to ant, mozzie and fly
There's a picnic we're hosting this Christmas
Masked up we're waving ISO goodbye
To the hills and wide-open spaces
As shut-ins we're finally out
It's wildlife and trees we're seeking
And koalas cuddly and stout
A true-blue Christmas we're embracing
Tho' a gathering small, only six
We're big on toasting good fortunes
Cheers to freedom and our Christmas picnic.

New Zealand Christmas Tree

Stumpy, is now its new name
Not because it was at all lame
It grew very tall and very old
Dropped branches with mould.
Over fifty years it stood there
Growing silently without a care
It did have one peculiar habit
When flowering at Easter time
It was a weird and latent habit.
As a small tree it was planted
Kids jumped over it in play
Youthful energy of their day
It never got a lot of attention
Just water from the sprinkler
When the lawn needed a drink
And a couple of light prunes
Over the years, clip and crimp.
Then it was left to slowly grow
Tall, and taller, higher than high
'Til it bloomed red at Easter
Topsy-turvy Christmas tree.
From my window it's a stump
Branches all munched away.
No home for the birds to roost
Or a koala to hug night or day.
Dogs miss leg high toilet stops
Gone the shade for parked cars
Underneath its shady umbrella.
How bright is the living room
Since the tree was swiftly felled.
Shades do help temper the glare.
Goodbye dear old tree, adieu.

Mend a Sock-Darn a Shoe Day!

'Twas the night before Christmas
And all through the house
Not a thing stirred -
Not a cockroach or mouse.
There was no milk for Santa -
And no carrot for deer
No turkey or ham
Or wine for good cheer.
The pudding was missing
And the iced Christmas Cake
You think that you're dreaming
But alas, you're awake!
Then you recall -
Tomorrow's 'mend a sock-darn a shoe' day
Making do's what you do -
After fire's swept so much away.
Celebrations are stunted -
There's no gifts for good cheers
So you take a rain check
'Til a better day rears.
You swallow your pride
For you have each other
There's no point in regress
No time to bother
On Christmas morning
There's a knock at your blistered door
You find a hamper of goodies delivered -
From your local charity store!

The Old Grey Cake Tin

This year as I trim
Mum's old grey cake tin
with its battered decor
that I now treasure more.
There's a tradition to keep
as I start out to beat
the eggs, butter and sugar,
flour, fruit and Madeira.
As the mixture I place
in old grey to bake,
I keep rules handed down
from a cook of renown.
Many cakes had Mum cooked
in old grey from her cookbook
which she filed away in her head
where her best recipes were bred.
Such tales could old grey tell:
how the fruit sometimes fell -
sunk down in the middle,
caused a fuss and a riddle.
How cakes rose to the top
and were 'cream of the crop'!
Or surprised - opened w-i-d-e,
with a crack no icing could hide.
That's when the bottom became top,
camouflaging the botch,
with a bucket of icing,
smoothed around before slicing!
There were good cakes and middling.
All were made with good cheer,
we each took a stir, made a wish in the pot,
for a Noel blessing and a happy New Year!

Quirky Hats

In darkness they're hidden all year through,
But come the holidays they make a debut.
In a very humble, yet humorous way
They help to celebrate Christ's Birthday.
Born out of a pop with an ear- piercing bang
and packaged tightly with a rubber band.
Their colours are bright, tho' patterns vary
One size fits all to make Christmas merry.
Grandma looks cool in her ruby-red crown
while Grandpa is sporting a curious frown.
Uncle Lou's hat has slipped to one side,
and Aunty Helena has cast hers wide.
Mother's not keen on the crowning at all,
Dad's wearing his and he's having a ball.
People try avoiding the camera's flash
by stepping aside in a half-hearted dash.
Those corny jokes and hats made of paper
have everyone laughing, sooner than later.
Such sights they appear wearing crepe array
Aping quirky mad-hatters on Christmas Day!

Gift Bearing

What did you get for Christmas?
Was it like or dislike at first dekko?
Did the thingamabob you were given
Smack with un-given grace as so-so?
How did you deal with this dilemma?
Did you fess up or bravely push on
Believing the thought's all that matters
And to smile in the face of hard done?
Did the monkey fart scent amuse you,
From the candle light lit for impression?
Or was it by way of a phoney pretension,
Masking as a tired Christmas expression
When you knew not the gift but the giving
Was the essence straight from the heart,
That it's better to give than to receive,
In there lies a lesson beginning to smart.
Finally, did your bottom drawer accept it,
To be rekindled again without passion?
Then gush at the unsuspecting victim
As you waited for a happy response
Came: Didn't I give you that last year!!
It's the gift that just keeps on giving,
So cheers and Merry Christmas, dear.
Tho' it's not how you need to be living.
The gift that keeps on giving.
Merry Christmas from the heart!

Angel's Prayer

Oh, Angel on the Christmas tree
Smile down upon this family.
Bless each and every loving child
As gifts beneath the greenery.
Hark go the wishes of the young
And present to every little one
A heart of gold, a stoic air,
Lest not forget a sense of fun.
Guardian Angel atop the tree
Hear oh this, my humble plea,
Shine tonight your blessed light
O'er kith and kin, he or she.
Aura bright, oh Christmas sprite
Touch all hearts so all will care
And give out love this special eve
To share with children everywhere.

The Wonder of Christmas

It's on again for young and old
The greatest story ever told.
The feasts, gifts, tinselled tree,
The gathering of the family.
It's church and morning prayers
Stay at homes have other cares.
Good, bad, those in between
Foster graces you've never see.
Grand if we kept this ambience
All year round without pretence.
A Christmas spirit for one and all
The good will tower and never fall.
The wonder of Christmas can be
How people share their spirituality.
Unselfishly giving and not whine
Helping others at Christmas time.
Christmas tree has wondrous bling
A star is close to an Angel's wing.
Symbols peace reigns supreme
And world love; is not a dream.

Nativity Oversight

A swaddling cloth,
Pale yellow hay
A new born baby
In a manger lay.
A little boy -
His worried look.
A pristine hanky
From his pocket took.
A fold or two
Then in a trice
A pillow fashioned
For the baby Christ.
No gift of gold
Nor splendid ring
Simply from his heart
A thoughtful thing.

Keep the Holy Christmas Spirit

It is the age old story
Of Christ child and wise men
A baby in a manger
The town of Bethlehem.
Oh, beautiful Noel saga
Remains forever young
Joyful in life and spirit
Filling our hearts with song.
Oh, keepers of the spirit
Closest in heart and mind
Proclaim the holy message
To comfort all mankind.
May the light of Christmas
Shine out from deep inside
The hearts of good Christians
Where love and hope abide.

A Wing and a Song

Brassy lilts in the air
Float into my head:
Hark, the Herald Angels sing,
And Silent Night.
Childhood memories
Wash my mind...
Grey city lamp post
Fuzzy yellow light
An army of moths' wings
Best time -
In a frenzied dance
To brassy music
Played by the capped
And bonneted
Salvation Army Band.
tootle-a-tum
a-rum-par-pum-pum
The tambourines play,
And tink-tink away
All beat time together
Beneath light and wings
The band puffs out a tune
While the onlooker sings.

The Greatest Gift

The only gift that lasts and lasts
Cannot be bought with cash or card.
It's so elusive, can't be gift-wrapped
Foolish to try because it's too hard.
The only gift that lasts and lasts
Is given from the tenderest heart,
With lots of affection thrown in
This gift is hard to pull apart.
The only gift that lasts and lasts
Is made from a very special mould.
Its core is mainly heart and soul
The perfect gift for young and old.
The only gift that lasts and lasts
Can be free and as gentle as a dove,
Or strong with a faith everlasting
And the most perfect gift is: LOVE!

What's Christmas Nanna?

What's Christmas, Nanna?
Well dear, it's faith.
What's faith, Nanna?
Well dear, it's belief.
What's belief, Nanna?
Well dear, it's trust.
What's trust, Nanna?
Well dear, it's faith, belief and hope.
Three things, eh, Nanna?
Well dear, it's complex.
What's complex, Nanna?
Well dear, it's difficult.
What's difficult, Nanna?
CHRISTMAS!

The Little Christmas Miracle

Pageant - what a cutie
The little miniature horse
Born to its mother, April,
Sired by Goliath, of course.
April was only four years old
And died before giving birth.
Her quivering lips told owners
To massage for all their worth.
A little miracle happened
somehow April did revive.
The toy-sized Bambino
Was delivered, barely alive.
Tho' weak and unsteady
Its life was touch and go.
Would the horse survive?
The owners did not know.
They tried to save the horse,
Had many a sleepless night;
To bottle feed the little foal
Two hour shifts their plight.
Expressed milk from April
Who was too weak to try,
Mother's milk was offered
Via a rubber teat, supplied.
Only five kilograms at birth,
Yet, Pageant had survived!
(Goliath was in a Christmas-
Pageant - that's how Pageant's name
arrived.)

Father Christmas Has to Be Your Dad!

Who said Father Christmas has to be your Dad?
Ours never owned a red suit, or white beard had.
Being a shift-worker at night put him out of business
So the role of Santa was performed by his Missus.
Quickly, she tip-toed all around the house,
Missing the loose boards that squeaked like a mouse.
Mother Claus crept into our bedroom to place,
Those crinkle-wrapped presents that made our hearts race.
We'd peek from under our covers, after she'd gone,
While Mum's familiar rose perfume lingered on.
The night seemed so still, only the noise of a drum
Beating inside our ears, said: Quick morning come!

Traditional Tokens

There's a mail influx and no shortfall,
Textually they say: Greetings all!
Designed to mirror a festive scene,
With mistletoe berries and holly, green.
It's a postie's annual, errant chore,
Delivering daily to each box or door,
From me to you and you to me -
Going to and fro intermittently.
Special cards gather about the house,
A motionless lot - quiet as a mouse.
Their words of cheer and sentiment -
Bring smiles and incite merriment.
Larger cards greet us musically,
With verses waxing on lyrically,
Performing tunes, we love to hear:
Jingle Bells and The Midnight Clear.
Lines may thin from year to year,
Some shy away, others disappear.
Friendships formed in novel places,
Help fill a void of empty spaces.
As the weeks roll by, battalions grow,
Cardboard soldiers stand in a row,
Guarding seasonal wishes on display;
Traditional tokens of Christmas Day.

Keying In

Ol' St Nick was on his way
Computer surfing in his sleigh
Going through the lists on screen
Scanning for chimneys unforeseen.
Some were round, some were square
Some were derelict and in disrepair.
Tall or squat Nick had to view -
The ins and outs of pots and flue.
Tight sometimes their fit would be
And tho' Nick dieted regularly -
He often wished that he had a key
To make a more accessible entry.
Prancer and Rudolph knew the score
And could trot and stop at any door,
Instead of precarious rooftop highs
Affecting hips and scraping thighs.
So, the elves designed a special key
That Nick could use repeatedly -
For keying in on Christmas Night,
No chimneys posed a barren sight.
Now the 'chimney-less' needn't fret,
'Cause Ol' St Nick will be on deck
With designer key to turn the locks
To fill those empty Christmas socks.

The Scent of Christmas

The fibre optic Christmas Tree
Has lights that excite visually
A chameleon in deep purple hues
Changing back to greenish-blues.
As I view this ultra-modern wonder
Brown study makes me stop and ponder
The simpler times when twigs of green
Permeated the Christmas scene.
Glittering shells, some painted red
Macaroni strung on coloured thread.
Paper chains which trailed forever
All glued and stapled up together.
Stars and moons made out of dough
Hung with holly and a bright red bow.
Streamers were cut from paper crepe
With fringes of cellophane to decorate.
Balloons all round would sway and flop
With a silver paper star perched on top.
A pine aroma filtered through the air
Evoking us Christmas was almost there.
The heavenly scent of the Christmas Tree
Seemed to exude a penchant for charity,
Awakening the good spirits, love and care,
Heralding in Christmas as a time to share.

Santa's Aussie Dress Code

Santa Claus has cut his beard.
It was so long, so white, so weird.
He's stashed his suit, so fiery red,
And lost the sock upon his head.
That gear's too hot for Aussie climes,
And after crossing international lines,
He'd notched up miles and different times,
Felt cold then hot, he'd read the signs.
He knew his dress code was passé,
And didn't suit the Aussie way,
So, his gear took on a khaki hue,
Now he looks a Santa that's true blue!
He wears flip-flops on his swollen feet,
And short shorts to cool his sweaty seat.
A cork-strung hat to swing and sway,
And keep the pesky Aussie flies at bay.
Six boomers pull his laden sleigh,
To rev them up he shouts 'G'day!'
They freedom-ride o'er rooftops high,
Listen fast and you may hear him cry:
'Ho! Ho! Ho! Merry Christmas! Ho! Ho! Ho!'

Online Santa

Santa lost his mobile phone
Such a quandary he was in.
He rifled through his Santa sacks
And through his deer's food bin.
Mother Claus grew testy
And threw her arms up in dismay:
How could you be so careless,
You should be on your way!
Santa frowned and paced about
Mother thought he'd have a fit,
The sleigh was hitched and ready
Deer were champing at the bit.
Rudolf's nose was turning pale
And Prancer pawed the ground.
'Oh, my deers,' cried Santa
'My Elf-line's not around!'
A tintinnabulation came
From inside Rudolf's throat,
Jingle bells was playing low -
Santa thought his deer had bloat.
The reindeer gave a snort and cough
And out flew the mobile phone -
Louder rang the jingling bells;
The elves were phoning home!
Santa's helpers packed the sleigh
With toys and gifts galore -
Then set off with a Ho-Ho- Ho!
For that was Santa's roar!
Christmas Eve passed merrily,
The delivery date was met
And Santa chastised Rudolf
For his mobile eating debt.
Now, Santa's into laptop mode

Deterring mobile-eating deer,
He gets emails on the internet
And can be found ONLINE all year!

Now You're Christmas Ready

Well, are you Christmas ready?
Have you begun to decorate the tree?
Or hang up the Christmas stockings
On the mantelpiece near the chimney.
Are all the presents wrapped and tied?
And placed neatly beneath the tree-
Where chameleon lights a-blinking
Make a picturesque sight to see.
Have your Noel cards been posted?
Or your Facebook greetings entered
To those who prefer online greets-
While others are snail-mail centred.
So, the turkey's stuffed and basted
And roast-ready for everyone to eat.
While the pudding's boiling steadily
You've made a brandy custard treat.
Lo, should your guests arrive early
You simply fill their glasses - tall -
With lots of cool champagne bubbles
And turn up the new TV on the wall.
Now that you are Christmas ready -
Lots of duck face selfies will appear.
In lieu of a mistletoe/kissing-bough
You have a broccoli-bough this year!

The Brightest Star

Like moths drawn towards a light,
Three wise men sought out a sight:
Where the Son of God was born
They travelled all night until dawn.
Guided via the brightest star,
The men had trekked so very far,
Arriving at a specific stable door
To view the baby that Mary bore.
Bearing frankincense and myrrh
And a basket full of gifts and fur,
The sages silently knelt to pray:
For peace on Earth that holy day.
Those Christian blessings still remain,
For all who worship in Christ's name.
The faithful pray for peace on earth,
As did three wise men at Jesus' birth.
As those gifts were offered at the start,
With a simple faith and a merry heart,
Our prayers will deepen and increase
Until the whole world can live in peace.

Cool Alert!

They're not average backyard chooks
Nor pelicans in children's story books,
Or penguins wearing black bow-ties
And not wise owls with rounded eyes.
They came in pairs each year in spring
And could those divas sweetly sing!
They'd harmonise in the morning sun
Until their frenzied fossicking was done.
Such special blackbirds - every one,
Who ruled backyards from sun to sun.
Always alert and with watchful eyes
They'd search for naughty gals or guys,
Then pitch their song to Ol' St Nick
And name the ones who'd get the flick.
Timed children, who were wise to this,
Held wagging tongues until Christmas
Believing they would get to have a say
And dibs cool gifts from St Nick's sleigh.
Cool kids were in, un-cools were out,
To be cool was best without a doubt.
The little black book, an unfair guise,
For ticks or crosses was no surprise.
'Twas toe-the-line for good not bad.
Lest un-cools were left an empty bag?
Christmas dawned clear and bright,
And not a single blackbird was in sight,
They'd finished work as St Nick's scouts
And no one knew of their whereabouts?
Mother had cursed them with a frown,
She'd spied their calling cards around:
Dirty 'dobbers' she was heard to say,
That's so un-cool on Christmas Day!

Good Intentions

It takes courage to be resolute
To be steadfast until the end
To walk the straight and narrow
And not be weak and bend.
With a New Year just beginning
While just a babe in arms
It's not easy to build character,
Quelling those tempting qualms.
Yet, I made my resolutions
With bright eyes and bushy tail
And hopeful heart and stoic mind
Into a brand-New Year, I sail.
Alas, February's arrived already
And I haven't lost that weight
But next month I will lose it
Soon I'll be a trendy size eight.
Easter, oh, my sweet tooth:
It's death by chocolate - I fear!
My New Year's resolution - well,
There's still practically a year?
August winds are so chilly
I must eat up to stay warm.
A few more little kilograms
Will keep me cosy in a storm.
Christmas and plum pudding,
Now I'm overweight I fear -
But I trust my good intentions
Will serve me well - this year!

The Proof of The Pudding

It hung about in abeyance
Clothed in unbleached calico
Confined to homely quarters
Tightly bound with string and bow.
Its rotund bottom was heated
To bubble, bounce and balloon
Until almost ready to burst
From its soggy cloth cocoon.
It had developed and matured
And once defrocked and plain
Made a desirable Christmas treat
Enhanced by the magic of flame.
When it took to centre stage
It brightened up so many faces
As the flames danced and died
Spreading joy to people's places.
The holly that once adorned its head
Lay on the tablecloth in bits
All the bowls were emptied out
And naught was left - not even pips.

It's Christmas by Golly!

It's Australia all over
And all over Australia
It's Christmas.
From Darwin to Tassie
And Melbourne to Perth
Christians are celebrating
The day of Christ's birth.
They've tinselled their trees
Gift wrapped special prezzies
And prayed to heaven above
For Yule-Tide blessings and love.
There's a hush Christmas Eve
As small-fry try to perceive
What Santa will put in their stocking.
And whether it'll be nice or shocking
Christmas Day dawns true-blue
There's such a fuss - a to-do
As children undo parcels and gifts
To reveal: dolls, video games, and kits.
Later, there's bon-bons and paper hats
Lots of Gran's warm-fuzzy hugs and pats
And kissing cousins aplenty to greet.
Followed by steamed pudding and meat
Champagne and Ma's spiked fruit punch,
As family sits together for Christmas lunch.
The occasion is quite joyous and jolly
With Noel carols, mistletoe and holly.
It's Christmas all over Australia, by golly!

Christmas Encounters

When love comes unexpected
Like a bolt straight out of the blue,
Disguised in unkempt raiments
It can sweep right over you.
Should you click with one another
Then it feels good from the start,
It's like a match made in heaven
You can't still your beating heart.
When it's happiness in a fur ball
That comes to move in with you
Then the journey that you travel
Will encompass not one but two.
You may marvel at this blessing
Which brushed around your shoe
Mewing at you quite ecstatically
While you search about erratically
For last night's pepperoni pizza
Still in cardboard not in freezer.
So hungry is the poor wee thing
To see a cat starve would be a sin.
Never mind your homelessness
There's a warmth in togetherness.
For neither have family nor mother
A captivating tale of love for another.
Some days are diamonds others stone,
Wherever you hang your hat is home.
Future soul mates met in a laneways,
Streetwise, but with no place to stay!

He's the Reason

Queues are long, tempers short
Last minute items must be sought
Feet are burning, headaches throb
Thinning finances make you sob.
Shopping trolleys brimming over
With food, toys, a bone for Rover.
Santa Claus is on his way -
To grant wishes on Christmas Day.
All in all, it's manic spending:
Christmas cards, stamps for sending,
Wrapping paper, sticky-tape and ties
And credit cards collecting flybuys.
Herald in the festive season:
Jesus' birthday is the reason.
Catch the fever feel the glow,
Tie each present with a bow.
Gifts of love for joyous giving
Presents make a pleasant living.
Gather 'round the festive food,
Tuck into the Christmas mood.

What Christmas means to me

Charles Dickens' Christmas Carol Classic**C**
Holy hymns sung with voices hig**H**
Relationships, a red nosed reindee**R**
Illuminated trees, bright gladiol**I**
Stockings stuffed with special toy**S**
Turkeys, plump and cooked to a **T**
Mistletoe, where Dad kisses Mu**M**
And plum pudding, made in Australi**A**
Santa's gifts for girls and boy**S**

Strength at Christmas

It's hard to find a balance
Between things good and bad
For Christmas time without you
Makes it bittersweet and sad.
It's hard to keep the dream alive
Without your good humoured smile
Which lifted my flagging spirits
And made my life worthwhile.
It's hard to face the future
Each lonely day and empty night;
To walk alone with only memories
After busy days so full and bright.
It's hard, my darling, to carry on
Without your tender love to share,
So I must trust things to memory
To find you are still smiling there.
When my load is difficult to bear
I recall how you bore a heavy cross
And stoically how you soldiered on
With a strength so very hard to toss.

Oddballs

Red, rough and round was an apt description for a pair of odd balls. They were at the same time as scarce as the proverbial hen's teeth.

Looking back, I felt slighted by their presence. I was expecting bigger and better. How trite my annual wishbone wishing for a bike had been. I realised it was an old wive's tale when my wishes weren't granted two years running.

I fetched my new tennis racket, and went outside and belted an odd ball against the brick wall until it bled. The days heat was unrelenting and to make matters worse a roast dinner was baking in the oven. How utterly stupid it was eating hot meals in summertime heat, I thought. Some traditions die hard.

Then the relies from hell began to arrive. After wiping off their sloppy kisses and rubbing my tweaked cheeks, which must've imitated Rudolph's red nose I then had to listen to their gushing and prattle, like I was invisible: *Hasn't she grown. Isn't she the spitting image of her mother?*

While I pushed my food around my plate, the relies ate like sharks in a feeding frenzy. As they slurped more amber liquid, their voices heightened: lots of darling calling and other sickly names were bandied about the dining room table with the same old jokes we'd heard last year.
My brother and I were allowed a sip of beer. My delicate palate convulsed and everyone laughed at my screwed up face. I bit greedily into some roast chicken to erase the bitterness.

* * *

After that, I made myself scarce, not wishing to partake in plum pudding and runny custard especially when there were no silver coins to search for; that being the only reason to eat plum pudding I always thought. Instead I viewed the Christmas prezzies again. Dad's daggy Y- front undies and Mum's wooden chopping board - compliments from us kids.

Then I grabbed my racket and balls again and headed for the street. My brother followed. We hit the oddballs around. Some neighbourhood kids joined in the game.
A couple of lobbers brushed the neat privet hedge near us and landed on old Bennett's front lawn.   Everyone gasped.

'You'll never see those balls again,' my brother shouted, 'he eats them for breakfast!'

'Just go in and get them. Mind how you go,' said Valery, from next door.

'Not on your life,' I protested, 'I'm not going in there! He's a modern day Scrooge!'

'Is that a fact?' A voice boomed from the other-side of the hedge and everyone stood to attention. 'What are these missiles doing spoiling my hedge then?'
In a kind of salute, Scrooge held the balls high in his large hands. At that very moment I crossed my fingers behind my back and wished hard: Please return my red Christmas balls.
It was then that a smallish woman sidled up to Scrooge.

'Give 'em back their balls, ya big lug!' She gave him a shove. Like boomerangs the oddballs, together, with my faith in humanity, returned. We clapped and ran about catching the balls as they dribbled about the roadside, before getting stuck in some of the melting bitumen.

* * *

Unwittingly, Scrooge's wife had demonstrated to all of us what the true meaning of Christmas really meant.No matter how small the gift or the gesture, it was far better to give than to receive!

Circa - Christmas 1948

Grandad and the Snake

    The old man was tired after his early morning fishing spree. He'd landed a bream well over two kilograms and his muscles were now objecting.
He'd been coming to fish at the Narrawong River for over forty years, first with his parents as a child and now with his wife Lottie and their children and grandchildren.

    He'd never caught a fish so big as the one he caught with the new rod Lottie had given him for Christmas. Well pleased with his catch, which was still in a net, he struggled to stand in his boat juggling the fish in one hand and rod in the other.
The boat rocked and he dropped the rod over the side into the water. He cursed as he watched his new rod disappear to the bottom of the river bed. He clung onto his fish, afraid he'd lose it too.

    The morning sun shimmered over the water. He squinted, but could not see his rod.
He wondered which news he should tell Lottie first: I caught the biggest fish ever for our Christmas dinner or I lost the rod you gave me? Either way it took the edge off his great catch.
A small voice broke his thoughts, 'I can see it! Bet ya I could reach it too!'
The old man's sad brown eyes looked towards the sound of the voice, to discover it was from his granddaughter, Ellie. She was lying on her stomach on the riverbank, peering into the water between the boat and the riverbank.
    'No. It's gone forever, Pettie!'
Before he could stop her, Ellie jumped in the boat stretching her arm over the side of the boat and into the

water.
The small boat rocked.
'Careful, Pet! You'll slip into the water.'
'I won't, Grandad!' She continued to search. Her fingers picked up one end of the rod only to lose her grip as the boat shifted.
'Forget it. I've still got the fish! He was happy with that and was prepared to kiss his rod goodbye, when Ellie squealed, 'I've got it Grandad!'
She held the rod up high for him to see.
His grin was almost equal to the size of his fish. He thrust a coin into Ellie's hand. 'That deserves an ice-cream at the very least.'
They walked back to camp, swinging the bream still in the net.

Lottie cooked the fish in the camp oven. She stuffed it with her secret seasonings and served it with salad vegetables. Followed by her homemade plum pudding, topped with cream from a neighbouring farmhouse.
With their tummies full to brimming Grandma Lottie told her grandchildren a story...

'This Happened a long time ago children, before we had electricity. You can't imagine that can you,' she cackled, 'they had electricity in the city but not out here where we camped. We were camped right here in this very same spot where we are now. Grandad was sleeping in a stretcher bed. We all went to do a spot of fishing and left grandad to sleep in our tent. Anyhow, while we were away, your grandad had a nightmare. He dreamt he was sharing his bed with some kind of a 'nasty'!'
'What?' asked Ellie, looking wide eyed.
'He wasn't sure at first, as I said he thought he was

dreaming. That was until he felt something wriggling on his stomach.'

'Eek! Was it a snake? asked Desley, perceptive as always. 'What did he do?'

'He called for help, but no one came. We were too far away to hear him.'

'Why didn't he jump out of bed,' asked Ellie?

'He was afraid he'd get bitten. He had to be still and wait for our return. The snake felt cold and slimy and as time went on it felt heavier. He felt faint when it moved a few times on his bare stomach. He was afraid to breathe too hard incase it disturbed the snake. When we arrived back at camp I popped my head through the tent flap. Grandad looked so pale, like he'd seen a ghost. I walked over to speak to him. His eyes opened wide and he whispered, "Snake" and pointed to his stomach.

"I'll get help!"

"No. Get the shovel outside and bring it in here quickly," sweat beaded on his forehead.

"Be very careful as you roll back the blankets. I've no idea what this snake will do', his voice wavered slightly."

'You must've been super scared, Grandma,' Densely looked awestruck and covered her mouth with her hands.

'I just followed orders. No time to be afraid', Grandma said. 'As I peeled back the blankets something sprung out and on to the floor! I stepped back and screamed! Grandad groaned, "What the devil was that?" Quickly, I turned up the oil lamp. It was plain enough to see that Grandad's snake turned out to be a harmless tree frog. As it started to hop away it paused and gave two loud croaks before disappearing into the night.

"Merry Christmas, tree frog," I said, doubling over with laughter.'

'It was a four legged snake, eh, Grandma?' The girls

roared laughing.
Grandad sat up suddenly in his bed on hearing the word snake. Shouting, 'Where! Where!'

Christmas Haikus

Ye Ol' Christmas
Tree Askew and covered in dust
Allergy hazard!

Ye Ol' Christmas Tree
Lay in a pile of rubbish
Fossickers recycle!

Ye Ol' Christmas Tree
Candelabra centre piece
dust busted festoon!

Lightning Source UK Ltd.
Milton Keynes UK
UKHW020223171221
395765UK00009B/687